christmas
cocktail jazz

Arranged by Brent Edstrom

contents

ISBN 978-1-70516-887-5

Visit Hal Leonard Online at
www.halleonard.com

World headquarters, contact:
Hal Leonard
7777 West Bluemound Road
Milwaukee, WI 53213
Email: info@halleonard.com

In Europe, contact:
Hal Leonard Europe Limited
1 Red Place
London, W1K 6PL
Email: info@halleonardeurope.com

In Australia, contact:
Hal Leonard Australia Pty. Ltd.
4 Lentara Court
Cheltenham, Victoria, 3192 Australia
Email: info@halleonard.com.au

CHRISTMAS IN NEW ORLEANS

Words and Music by JOE VAN WINKLE
and DICK SHERMAN

Moderate Swing

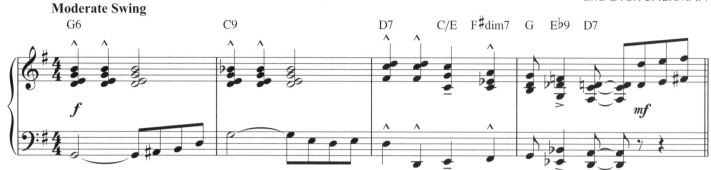

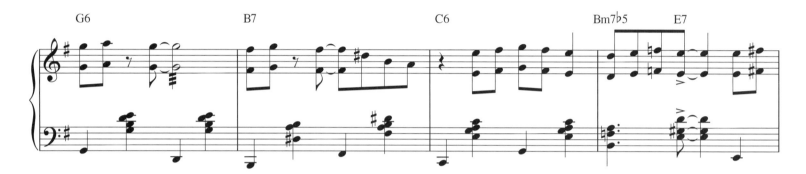

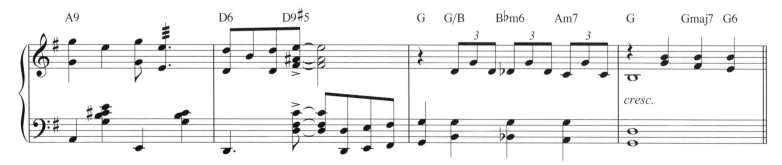

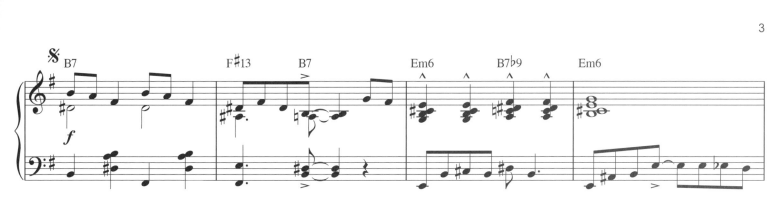

4

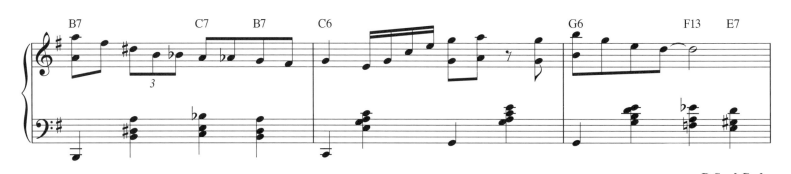

D.S. al Coda

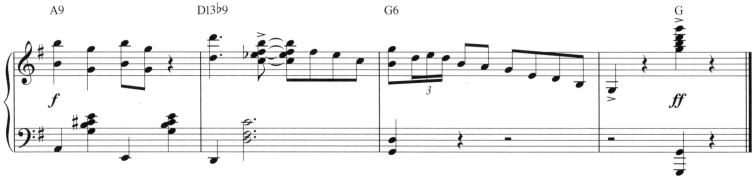

THE CHRISTMAS SONG
(Chestnuts Roasting on an Open Fire)

Music and Lyric by MEL TORMÉ
and ROBERT WELLS

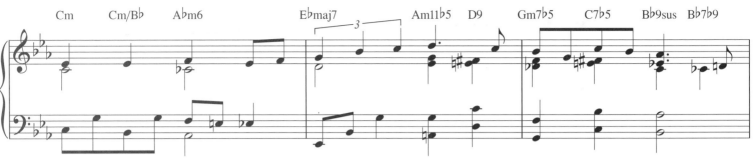

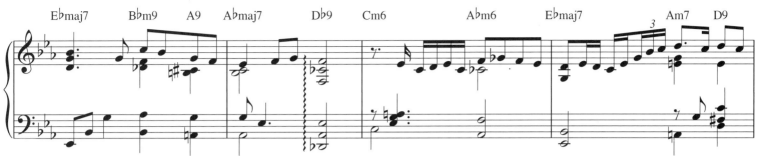

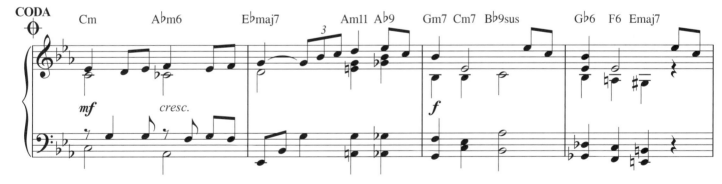

CHRISTMAS ISLAND

Words and Music by
LYLE MORAINE

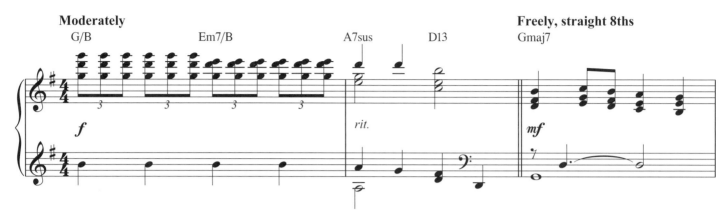

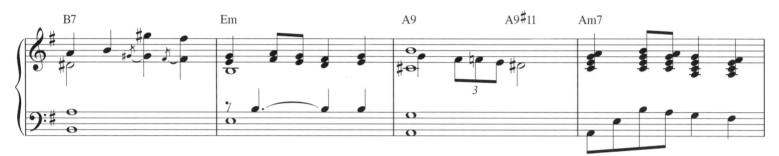

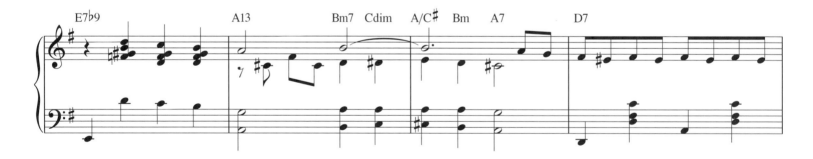

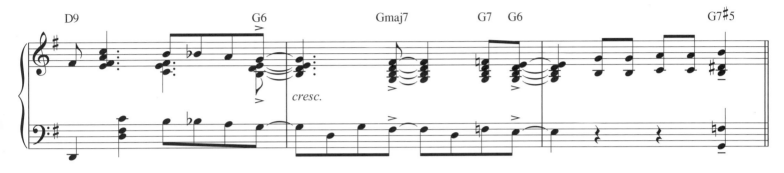

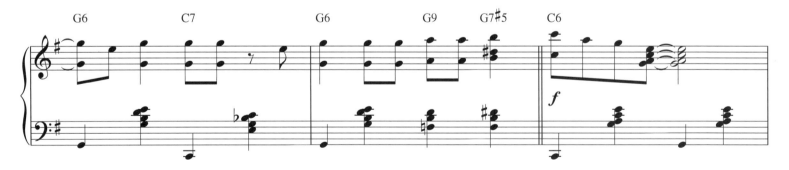

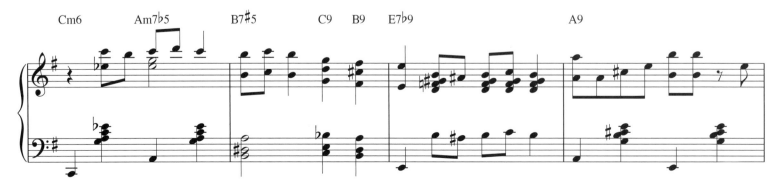

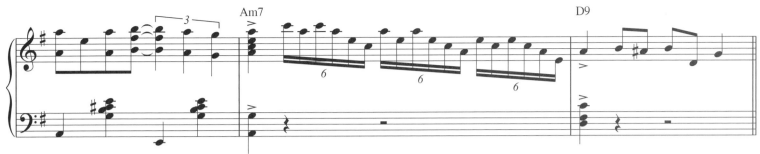

CHRISTMAS TIME IS HERE
from A CHARLIE BROWN CHRISTMAS

Words by LEE MENDELSON
Music by VINCE GUARALDI

Slowly

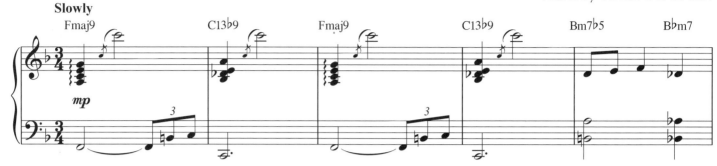

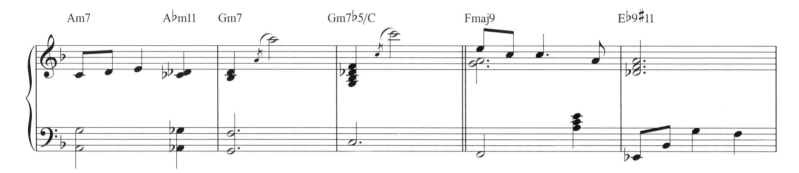

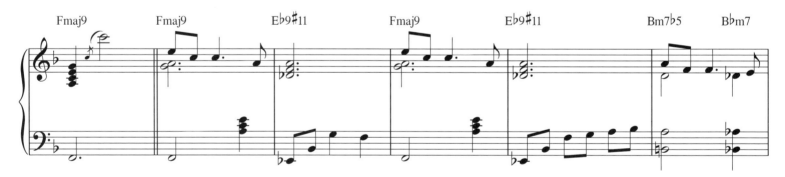

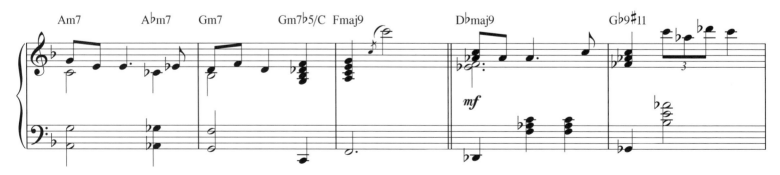

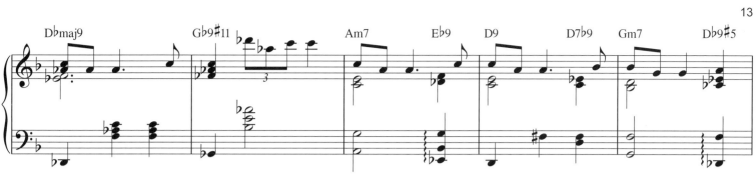

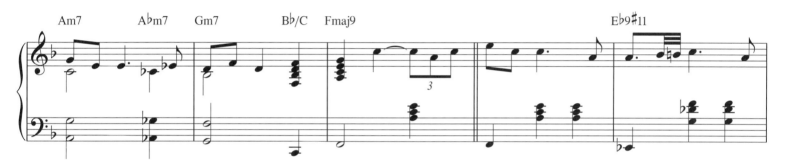

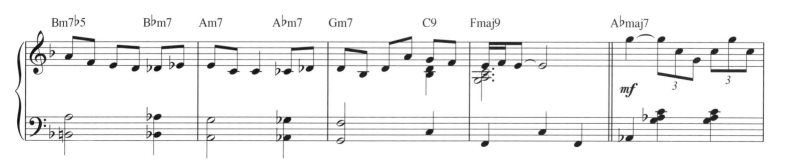

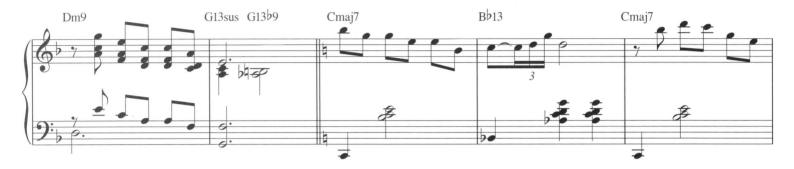

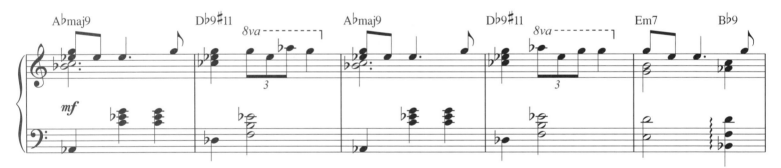

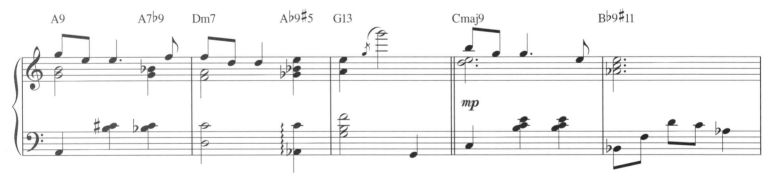

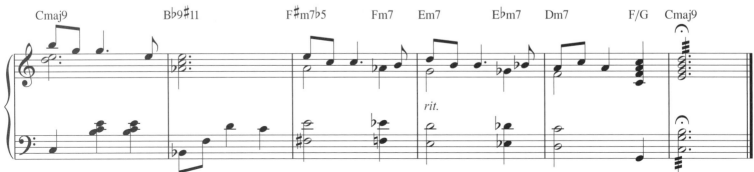

HAVE YOURSELF A MERRY LITTLE CHRISTMAS

from MEET ME IN ST. LOUIS

Words and Music by HUGH MARTIN
and RALPH BLANE

Freely, straight 8ths

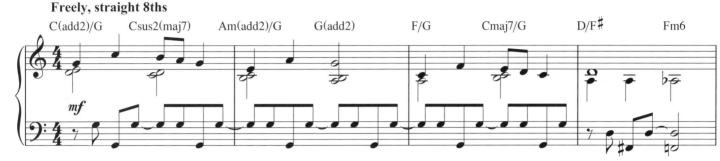

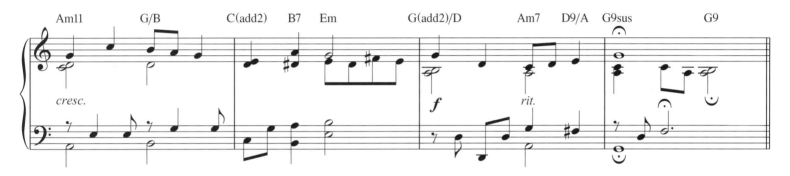

Gentle Latin groove

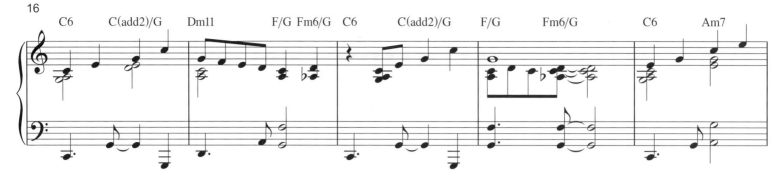

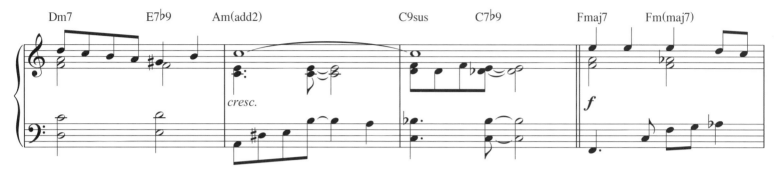

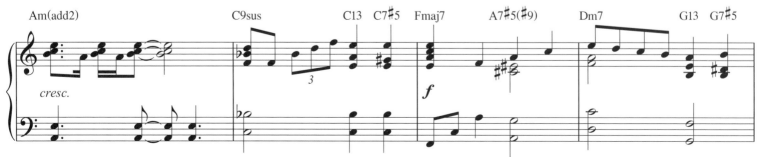

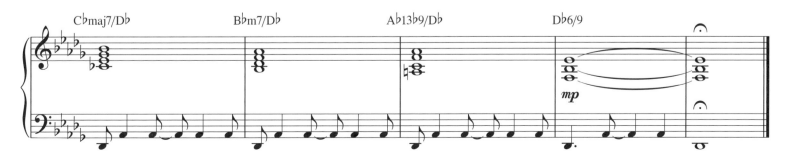

COOL YULE

Words and Music by
STEVE ALLEN

Moderately fast Swing

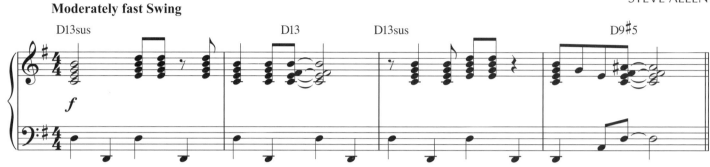

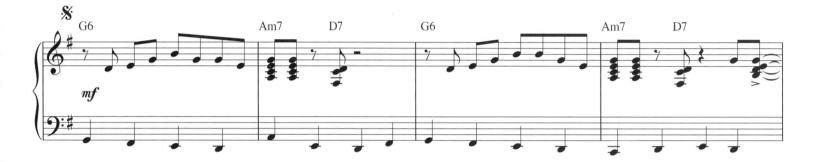

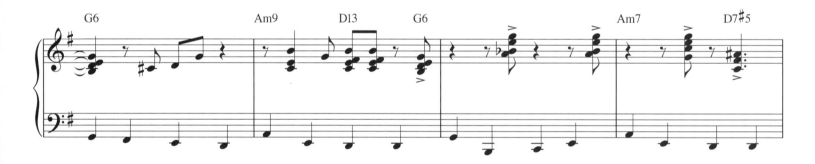

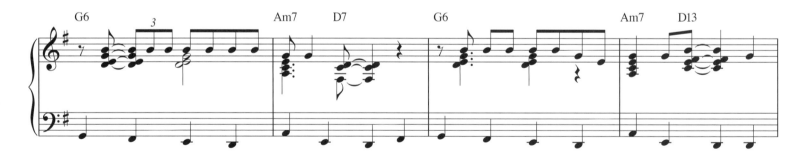

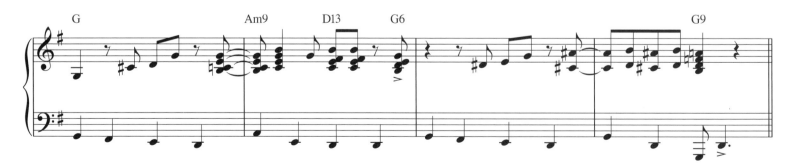

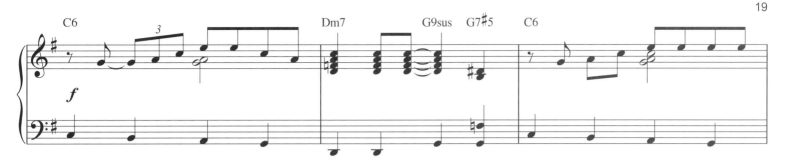

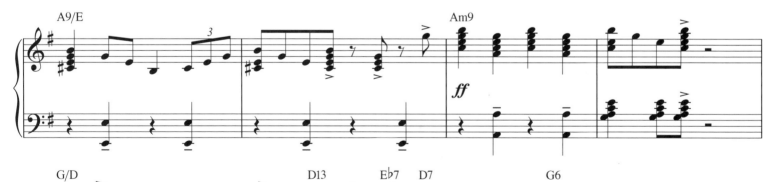

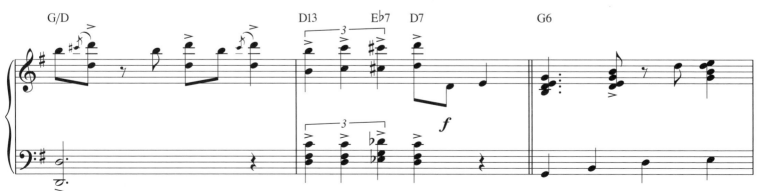

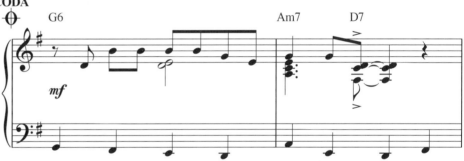

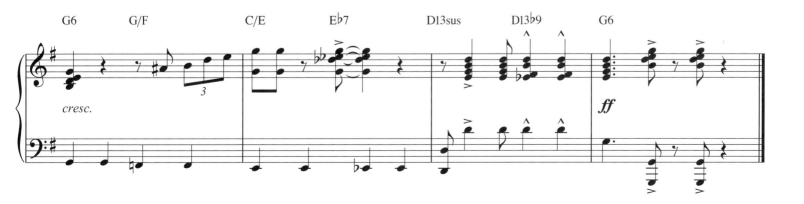

FROSTY THE SNOW MAN

Words and Music by STEVE NELSON
and JACK ROLLINS

Bright Swing

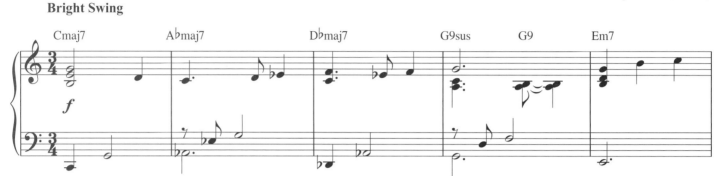

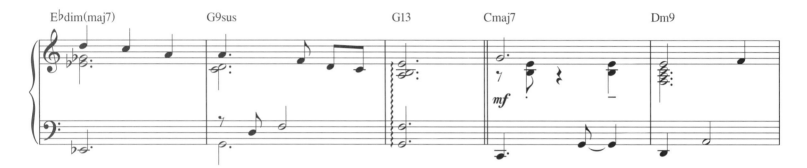

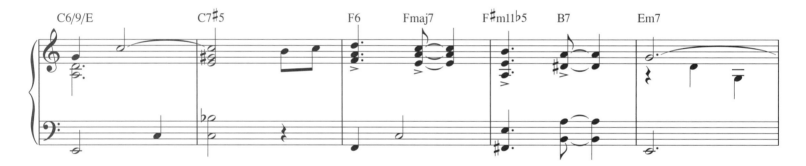

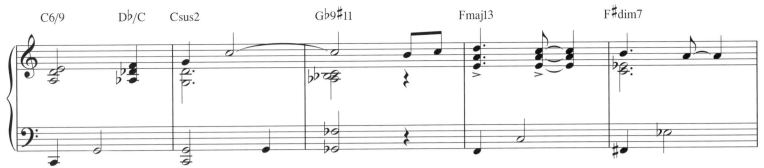

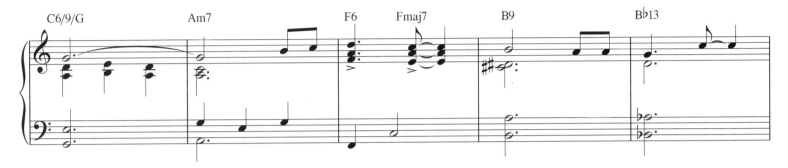

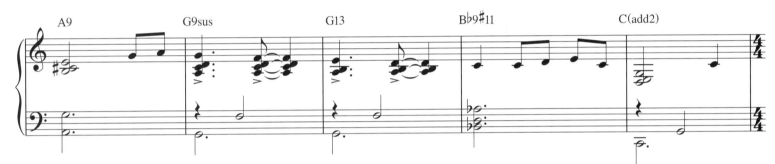

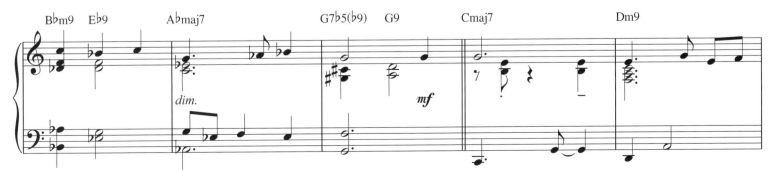

24

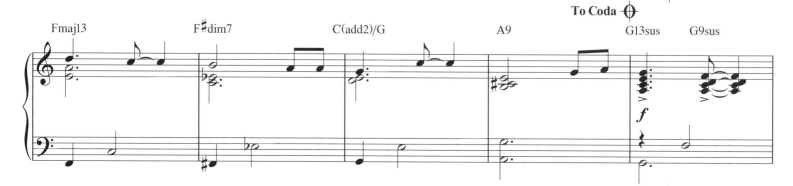

To Coda ⊕

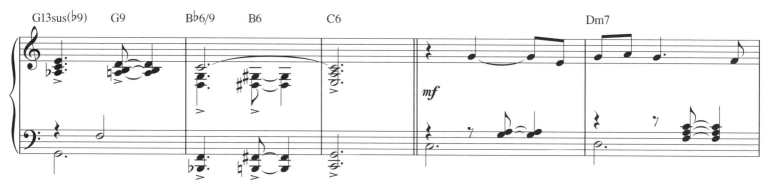

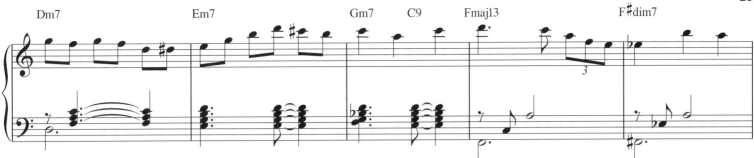

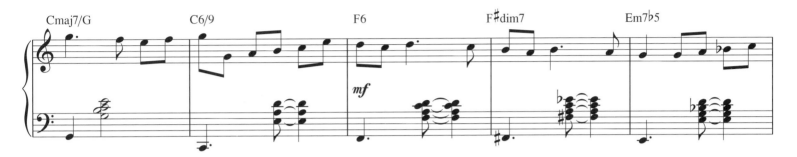

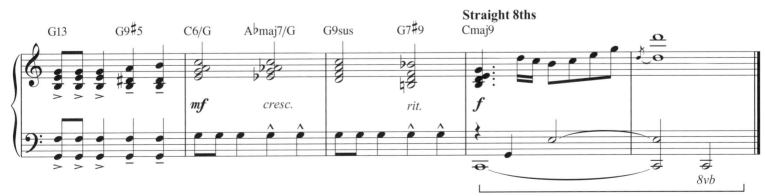

(There's No Place Like)
HOME FOR THE HOLIDAYS

Words and Music by AL STILLMAN
and ROBERT ALLEN

Gentle Bossa Nova

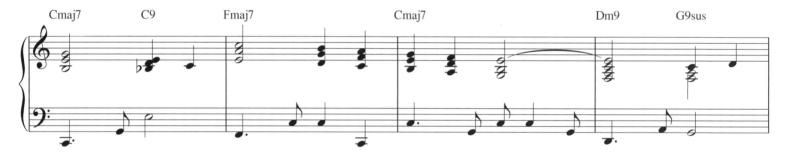

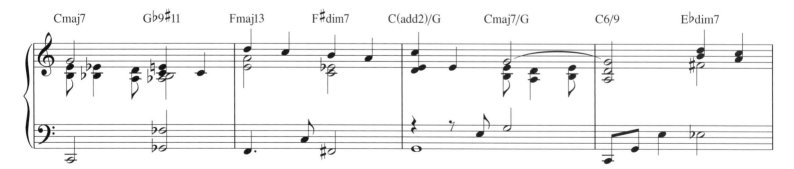

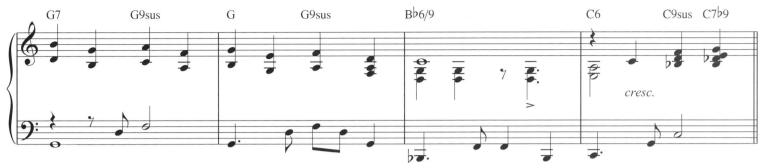

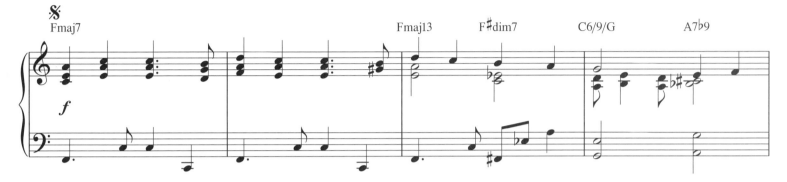

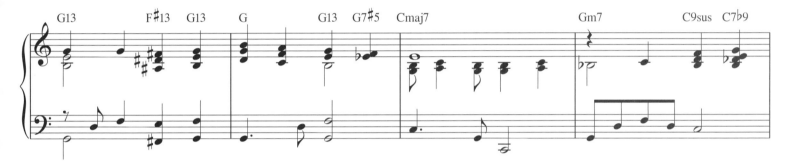

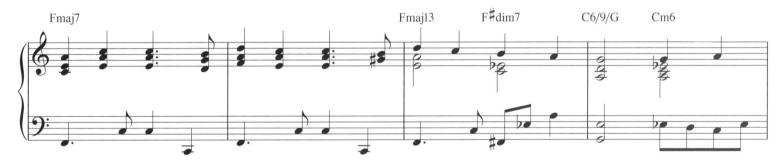

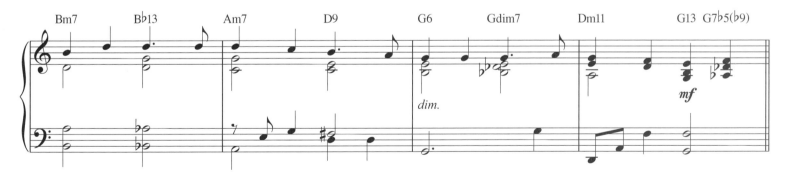

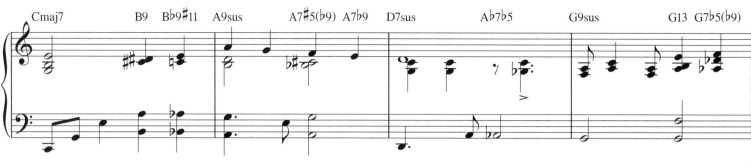

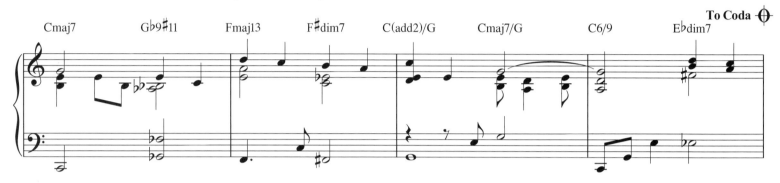

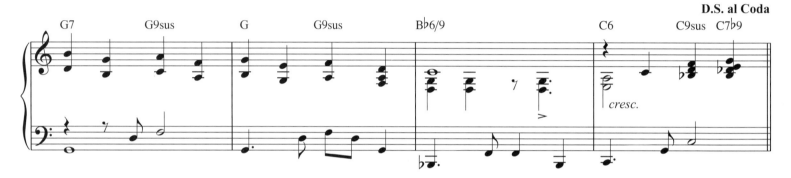

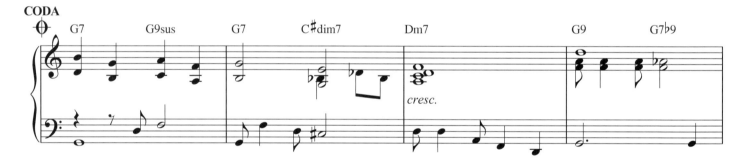

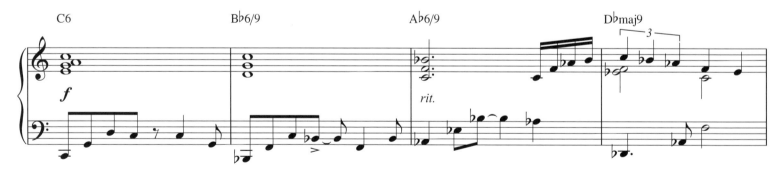

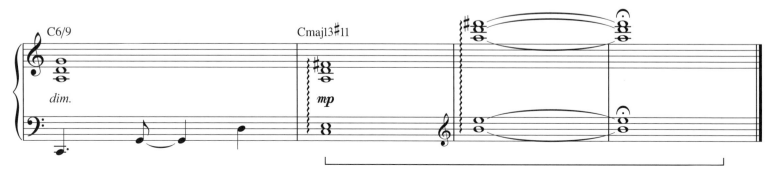

I LOVE THE WINTER WEATHER

Words and Music by TICKER FREEMAN
and WALTER BROWN

Moderately slow Swing

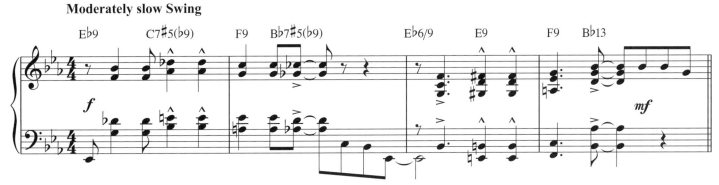

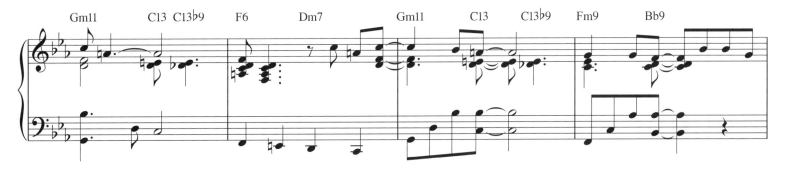

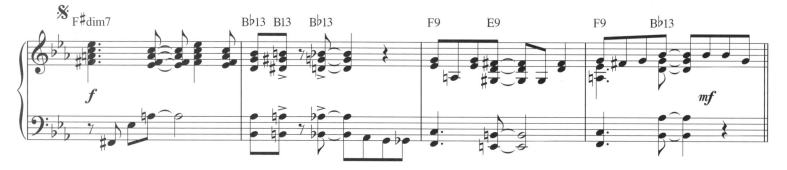

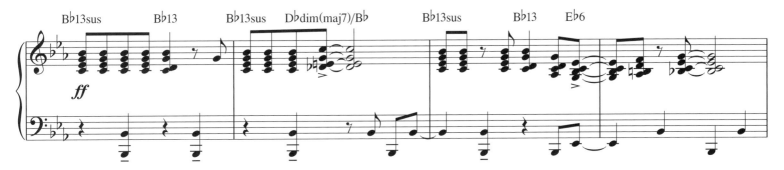

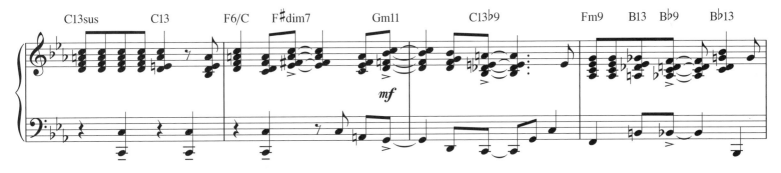

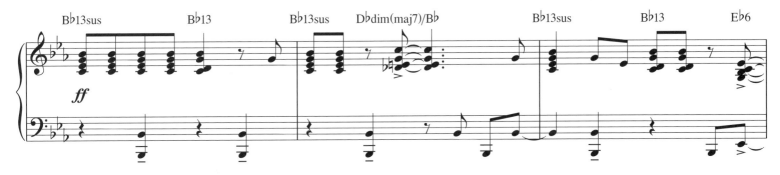

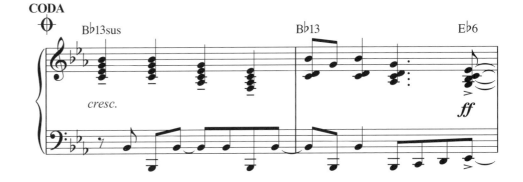

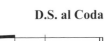

I'LL BE HOME FOR CHRISTMAS

Words and Music by KIM GANNON
and WALTER KENT

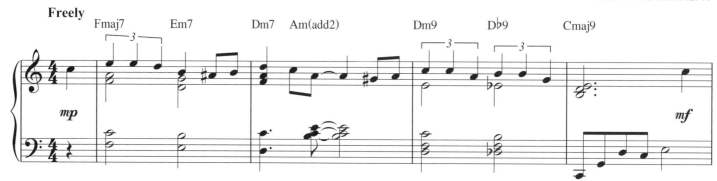

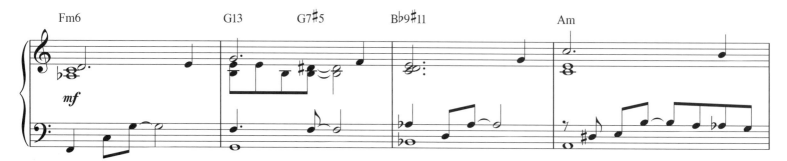

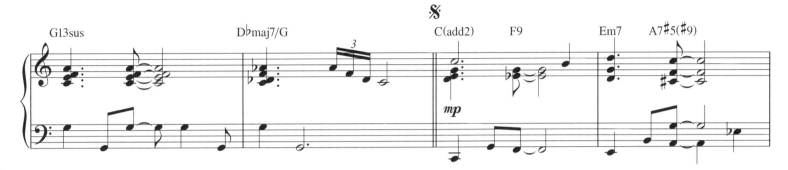

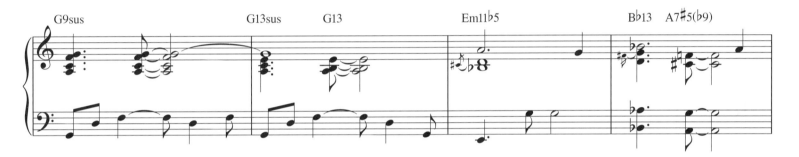

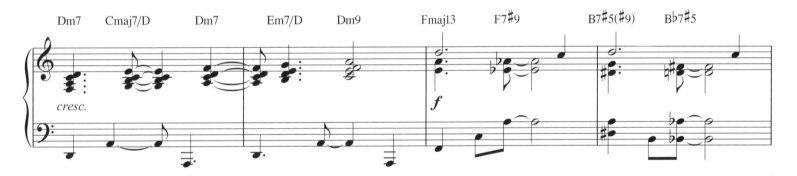

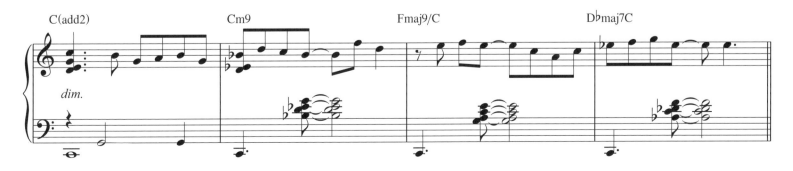

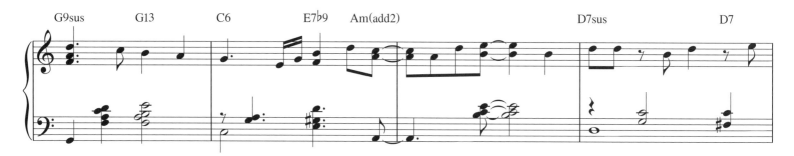

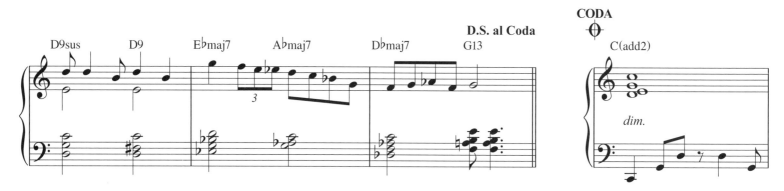

I'VE GOT MY LOVE TO KEEP ME WARM

from the 20th Century Fox Motion Picture ON THE AVENUE

Words and Music by
IRVING BERLIN

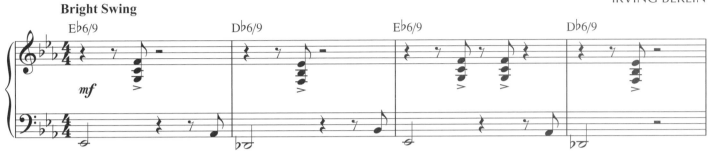

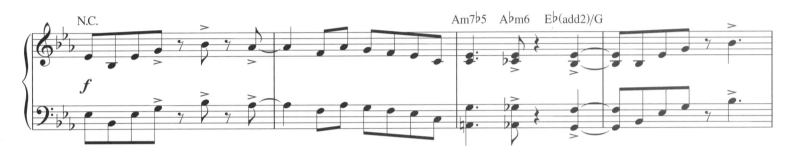

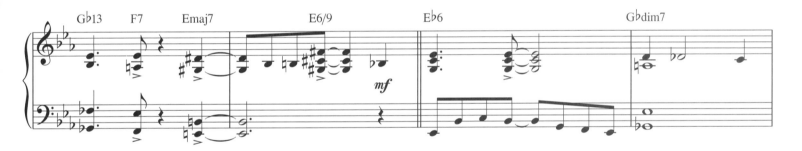

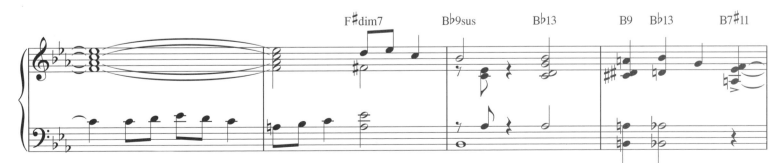

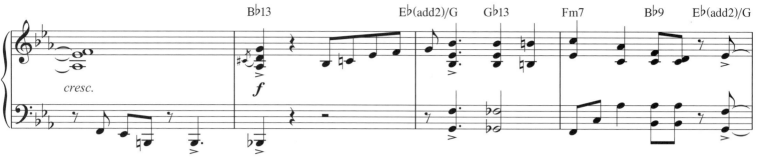

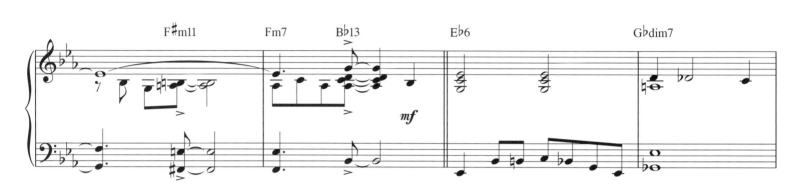

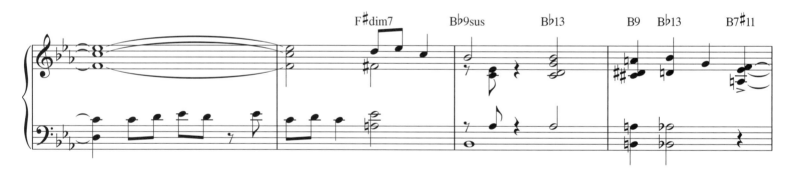

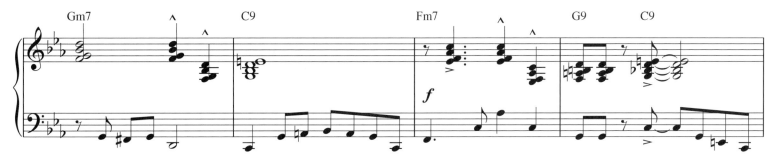

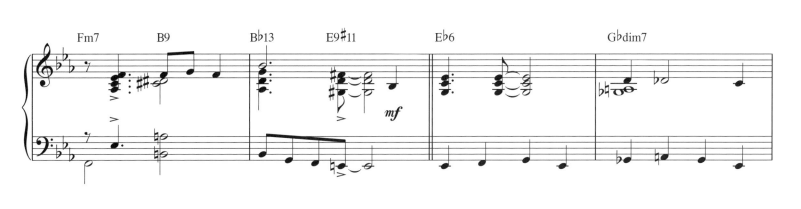

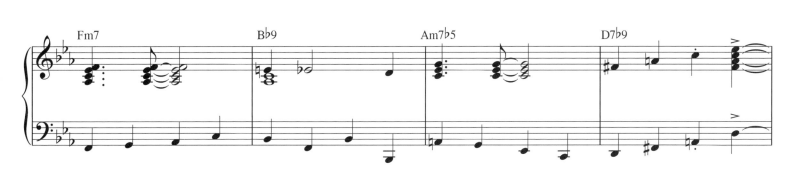

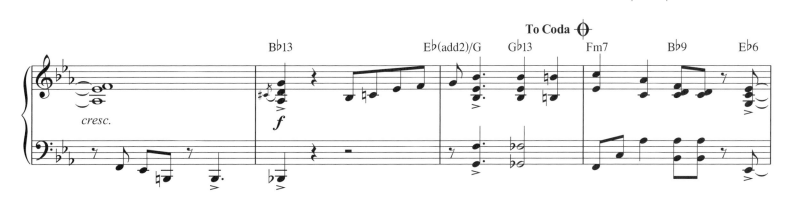

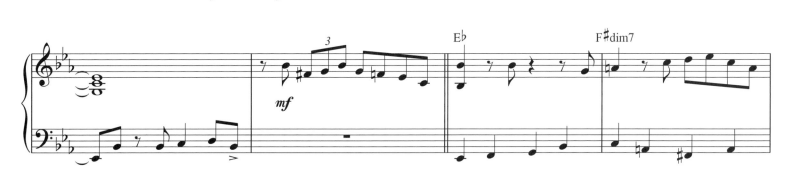

38

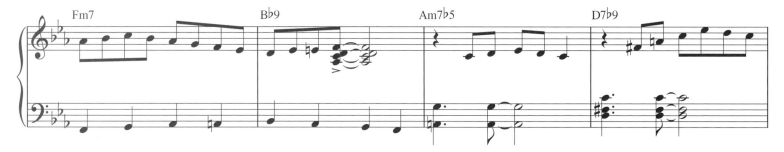

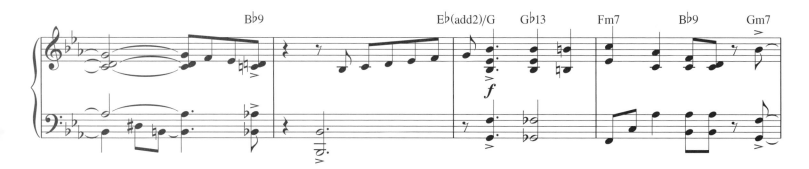

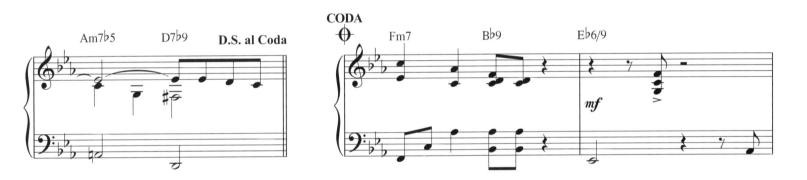

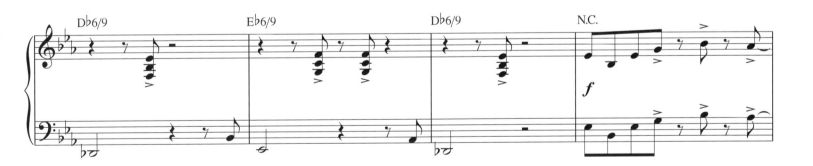

IT'S BEGINNING TO LOOK LIKE CHRISTMAS

By MEREDITH WILLSON

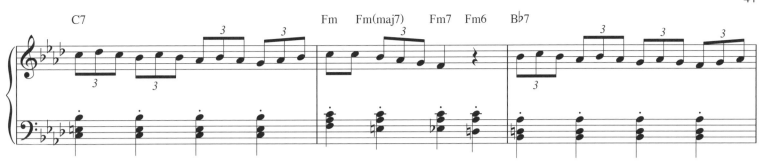

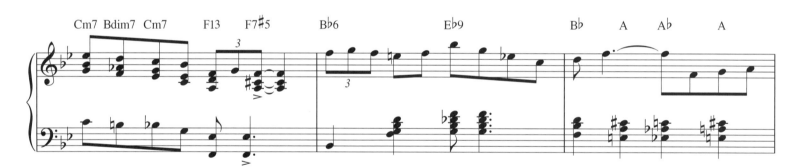

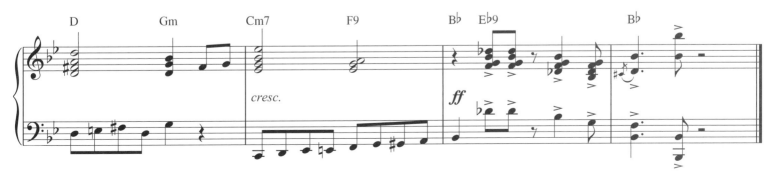

LET IT SNOW! LET IT SNOW! LET IT SNOW!

Words by SAMMY CAHN
Music by JULE STYNE

Moderate Swing

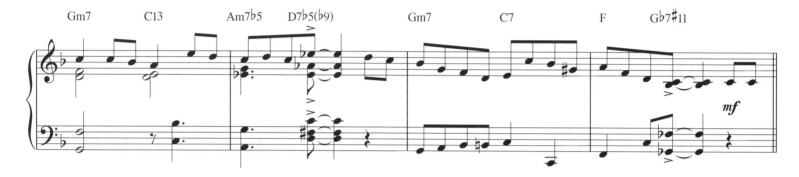

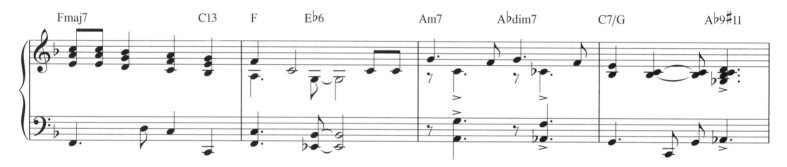

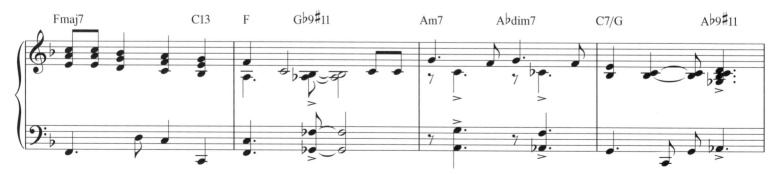

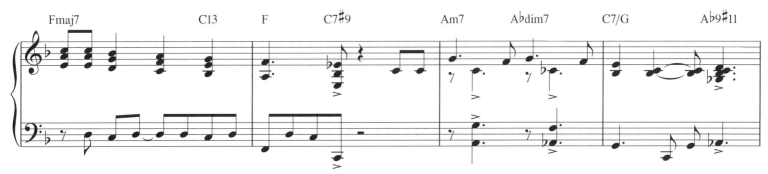

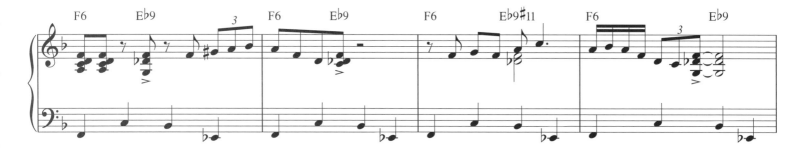

D.S. al Coda

CODA

(Everybody's Waitin' For)
THE MAN WITH THE BAG

Words and Music by HAROLD STANLEY,
IRVING TAYLOR and DUDLEY BROOKS

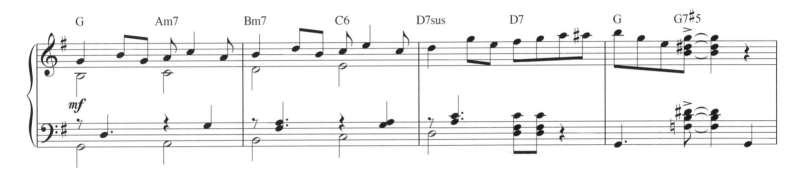

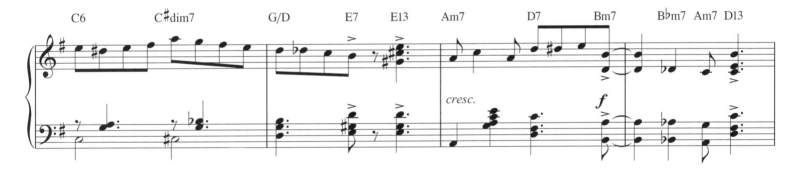

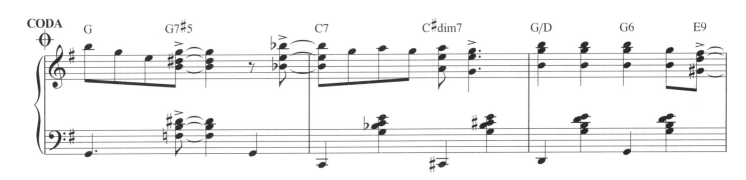

MERRY CHRISTMAS, BABY

Words and Music by LOU BAXTER
and JOHNNY MOORE

Slow Swing

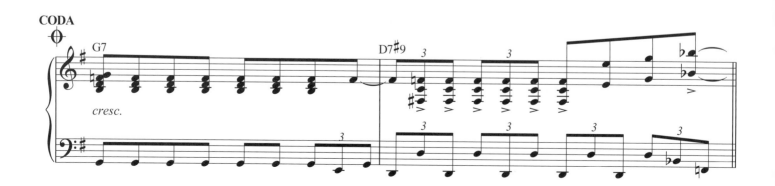

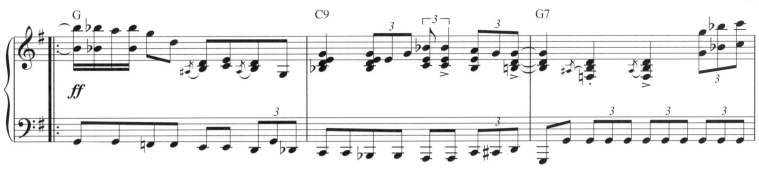

THE MOST WONDERFUL TIME OF THE YEAR

Words and Music by EDDIE POLA
and GEORGE WYLE

Easy Swing

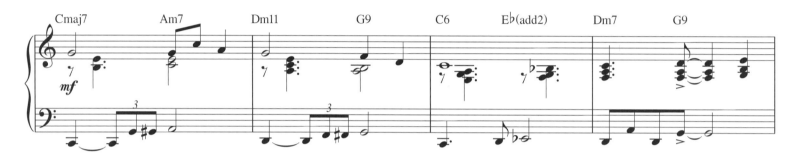

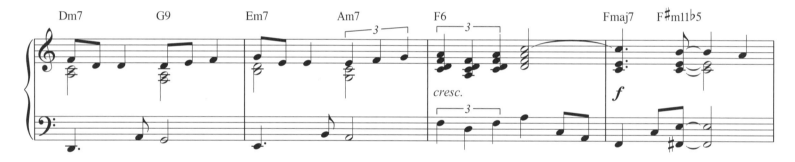

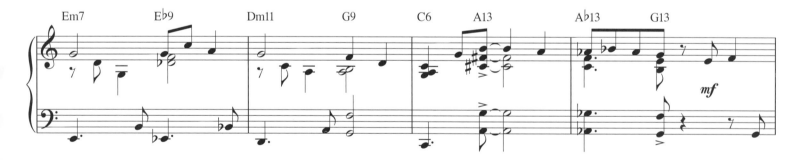

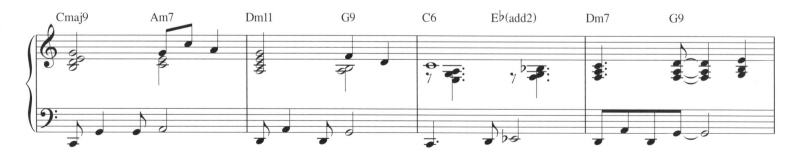

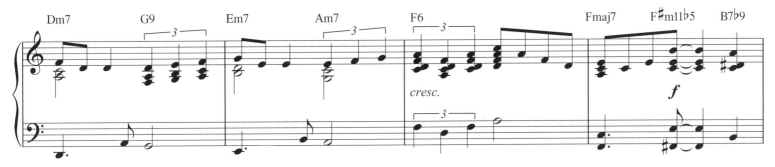

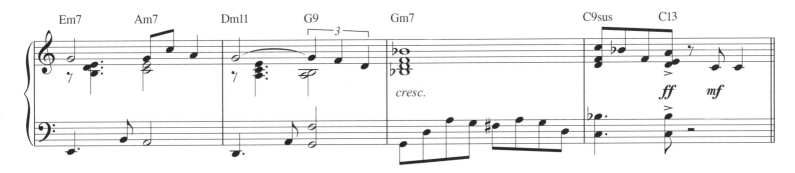

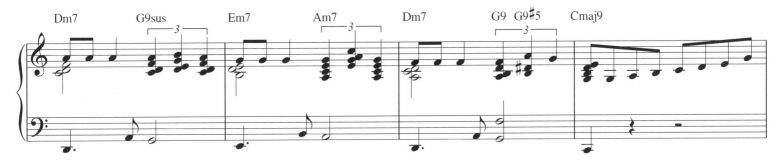

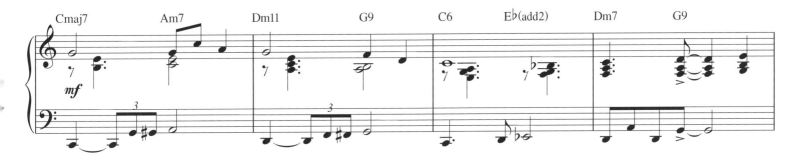

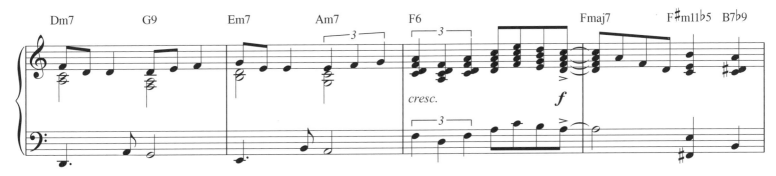

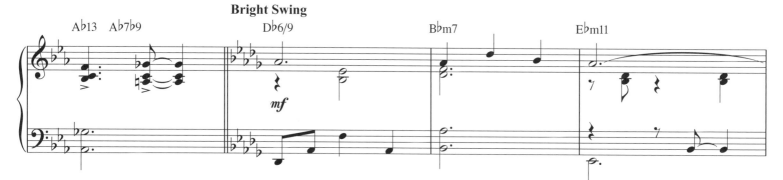

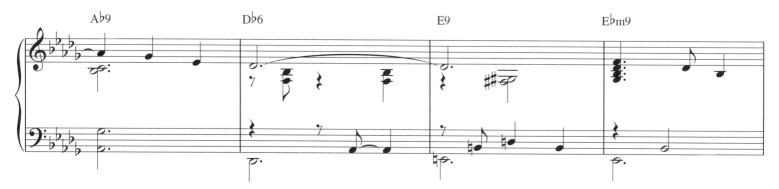

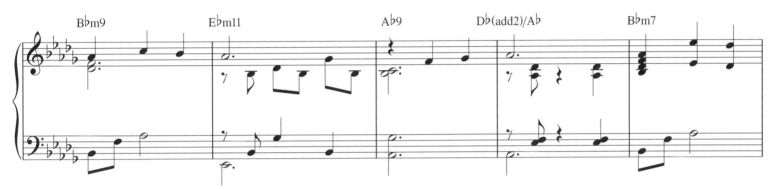

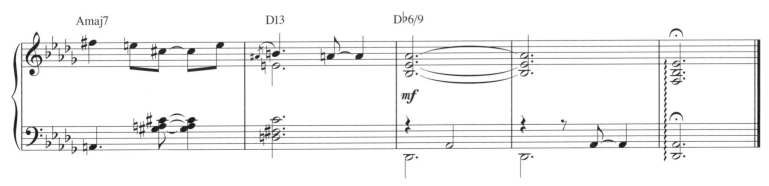

RUDOLPH THE RED-NOSED REINDEER

Music and Lyrics by
JOHNNY MARKS

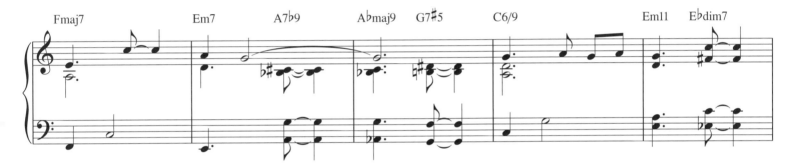

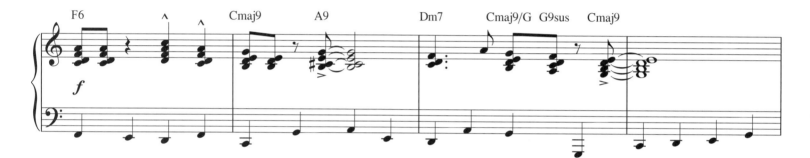

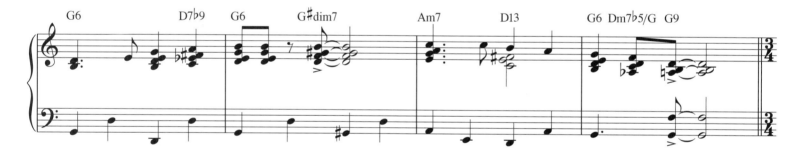

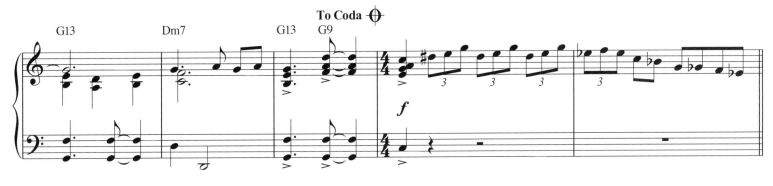

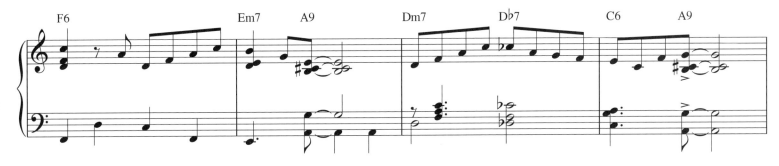

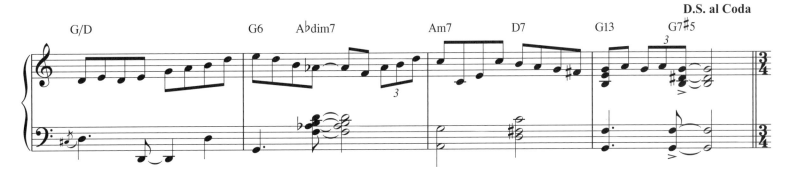

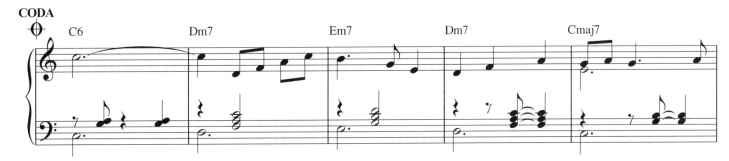

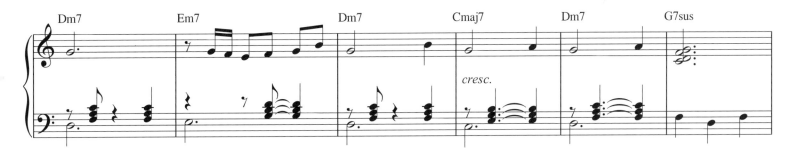

SANTA BABY

By JOAN JAVITS,
PHIL SPRINGER and TONY SPRINGER

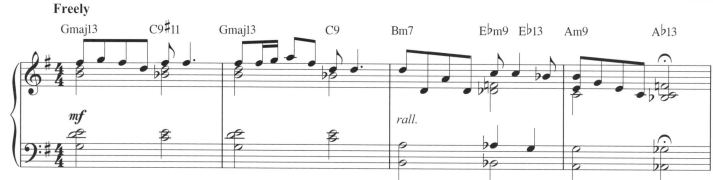

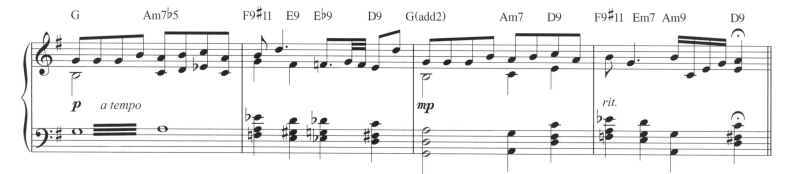

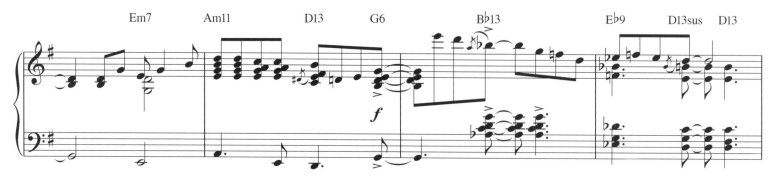

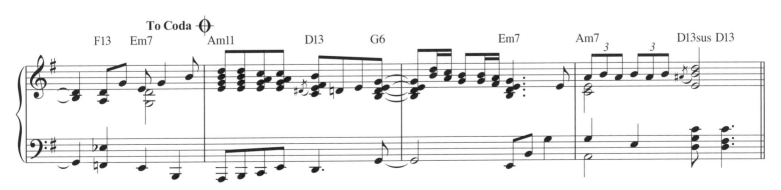

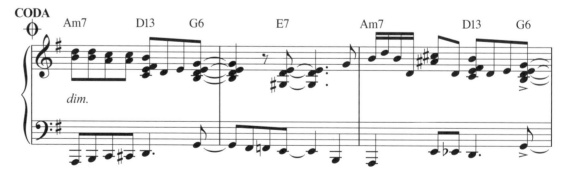

SANTA CLAUS IS BACK IN TOWN

Words and Music by JERRY LEIBER
and MIKE STOLLER

Moderately slow Swing

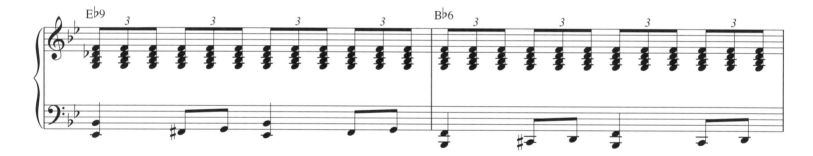

SANTA CLAUS IS COMIN' TO TOWN

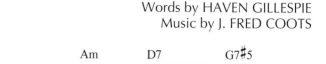

Words by HAVEN GILLESPIE
Music by J. FRED COOTS

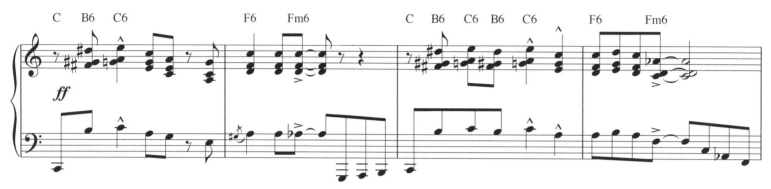

SILVER BELLS
from the Paramount Picture THE LEMON DROP KID

Words and Music by JAY LIVINGSTON
and RAY EVANS

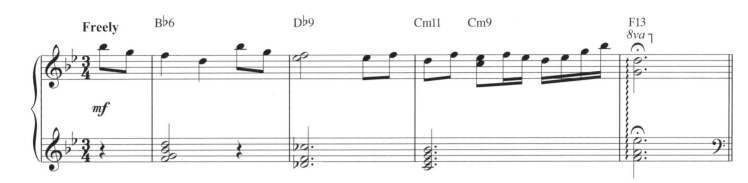

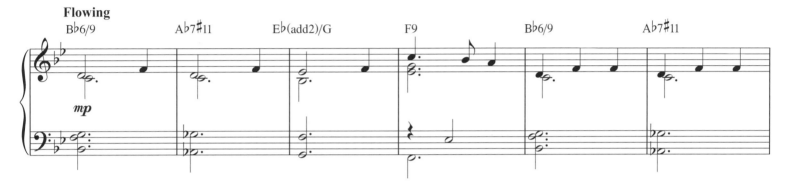

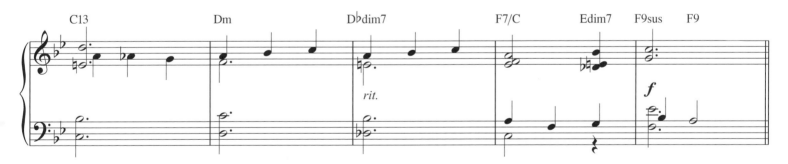

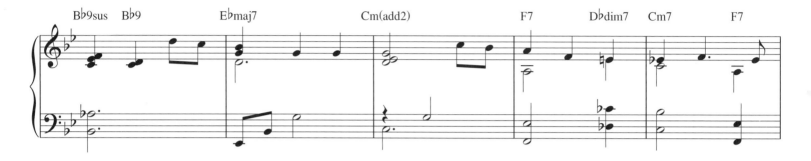

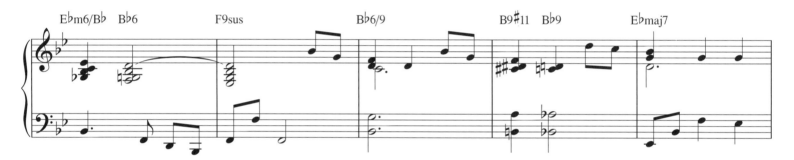

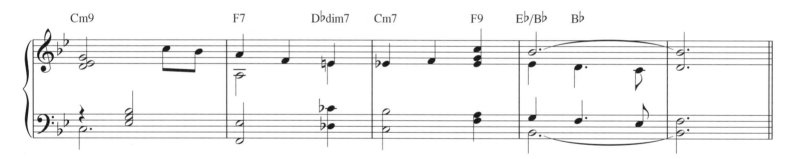

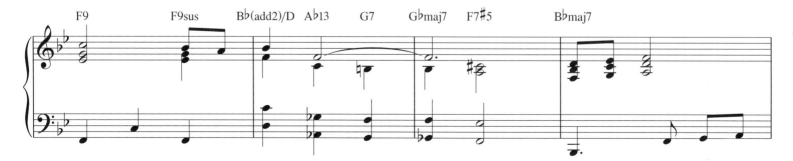

THE SECRET OF CHRISTMAS

Words by SAMMY CAHN
Music by JAMES VAN HEUSEN

Easy Latin groove

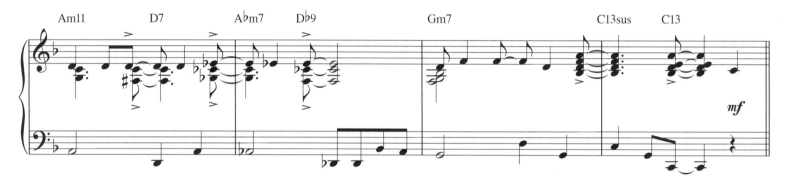

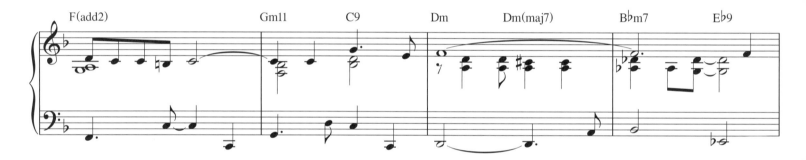

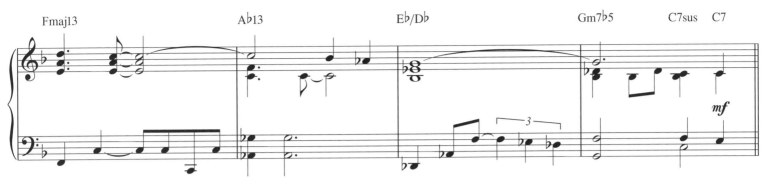

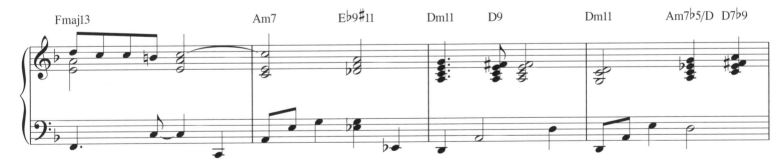

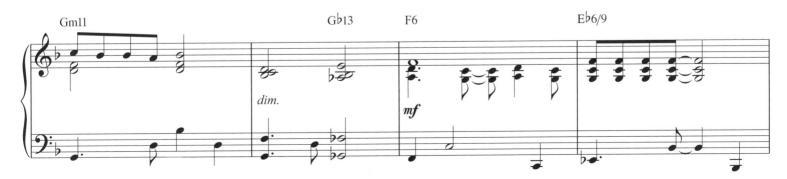

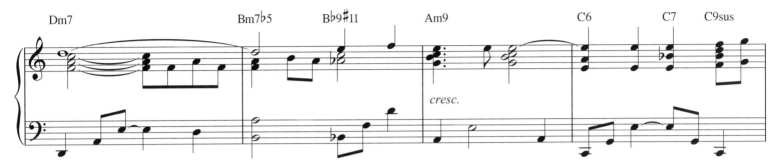

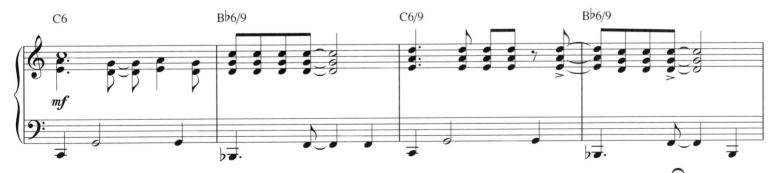

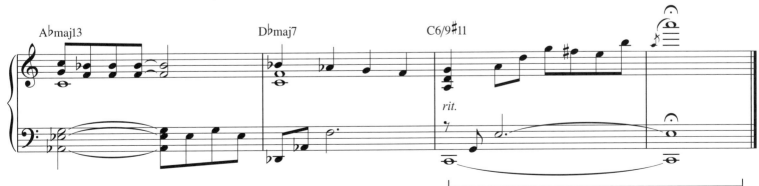

THAT'S WHAT I WANT FOR CHRISTMAS

Words and Music by
E.E. LAWRENCE

Slowly, with expression

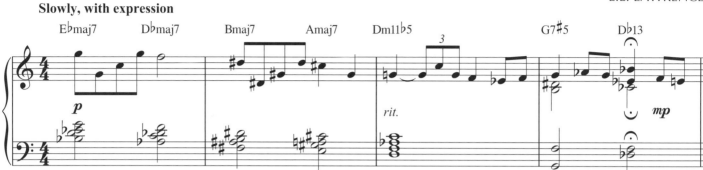

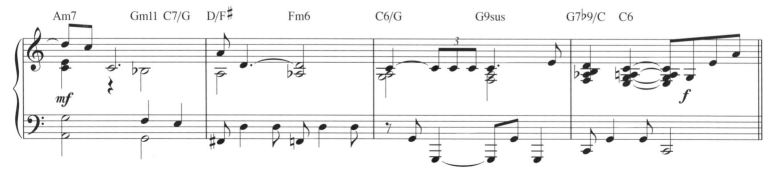

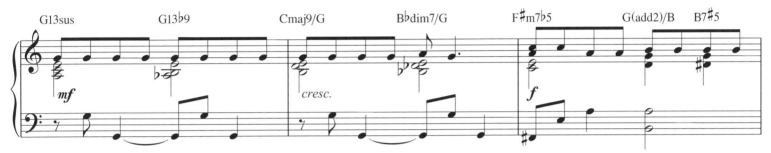

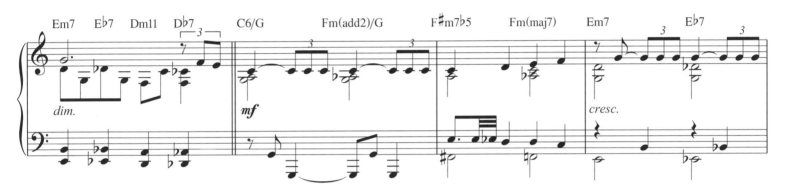

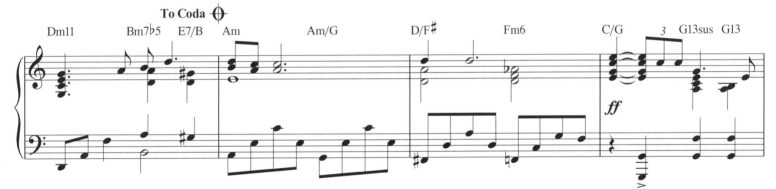

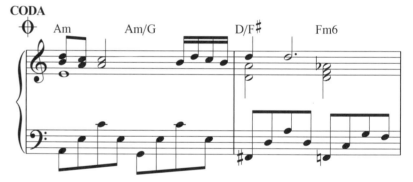

WHAT ARE YOU DOING NEW YEAR'S EVE?

By FRANK LOESSER

Moderately slow Swing

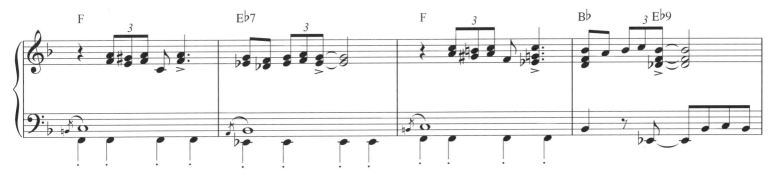

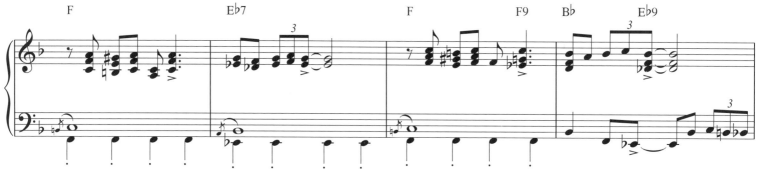

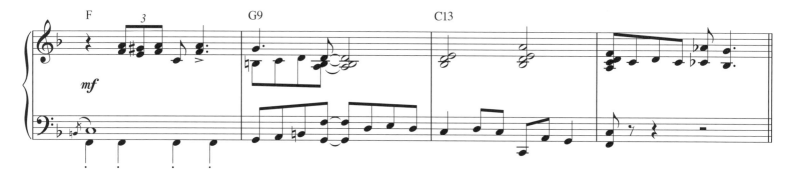

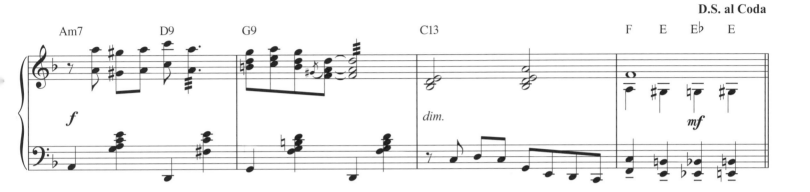

D.S. al Coda

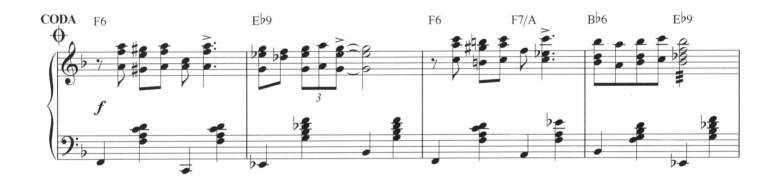

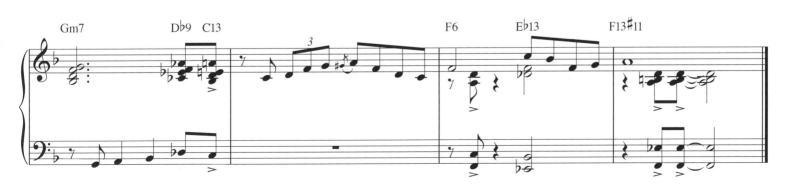

WE WISH YOU THE MERRIEST

Words and Music by
LES BROWN

Moderately fast Swing

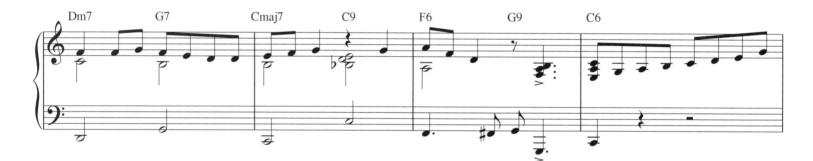

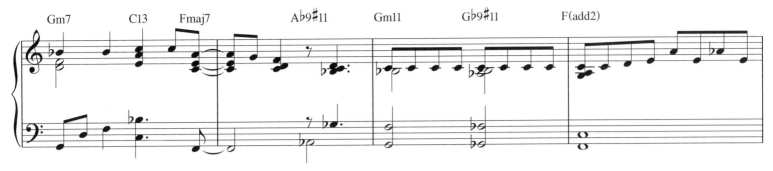

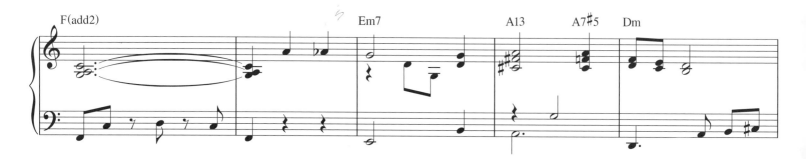

WHITE CHRISTMAS
from the Motion Picture Irving Berlin's HOLIDAY INN

Words and Music by
IRVING BERLIN

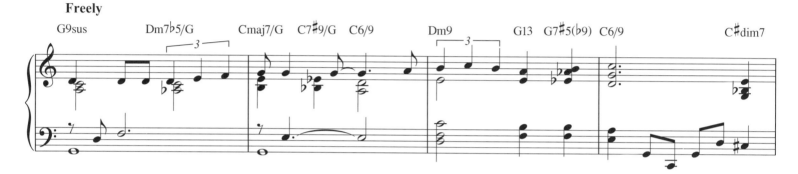

Moderately slow bluesy Swing

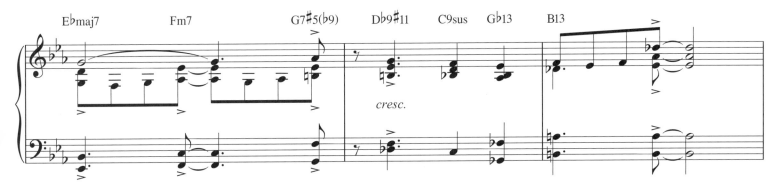

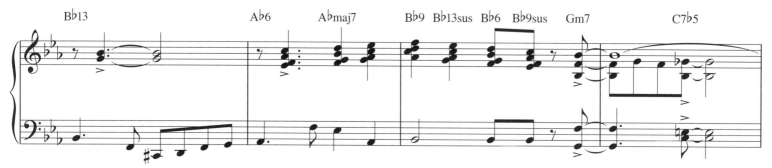

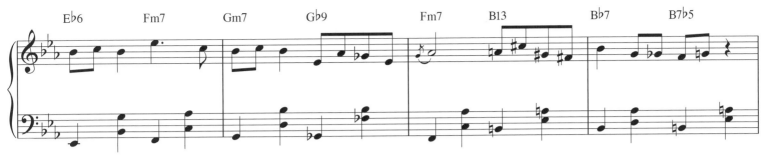

'ZAT YOU, SANTA CLAUS?

Words and Music by
JACK FOX

Moderately slow Swing

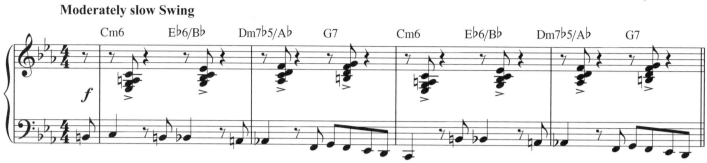

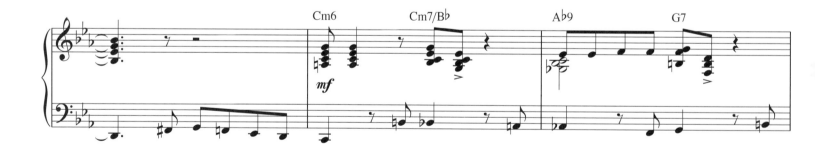

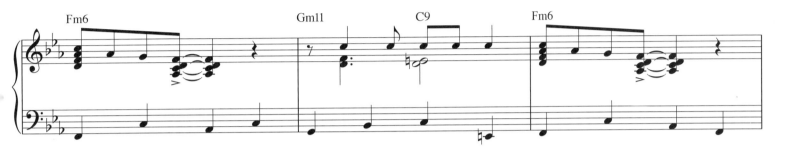

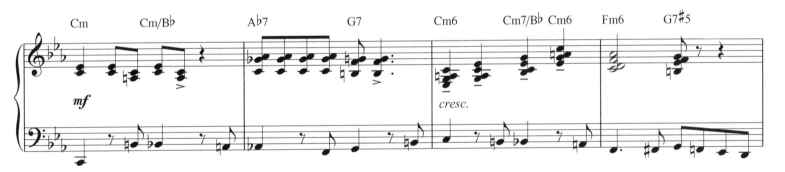

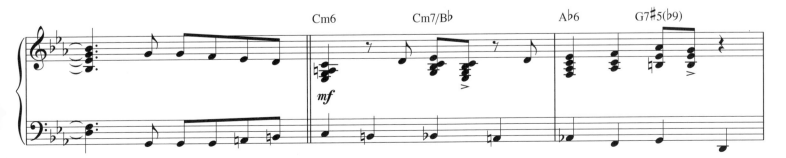

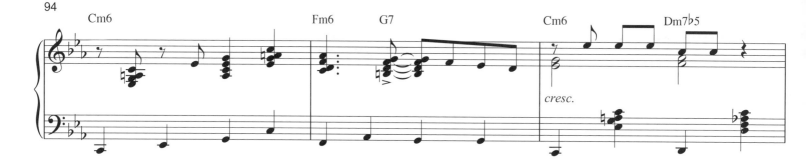

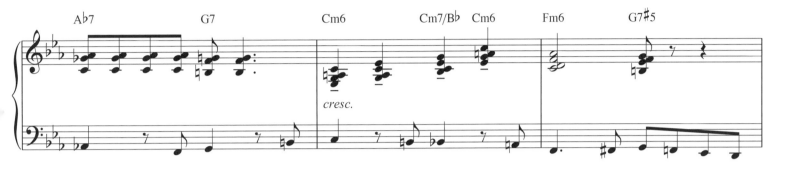

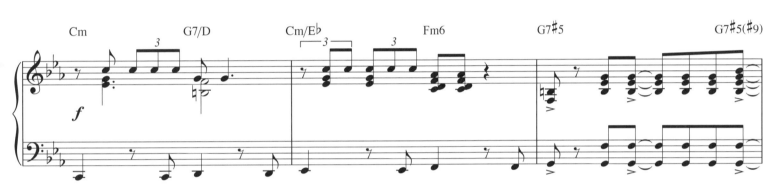

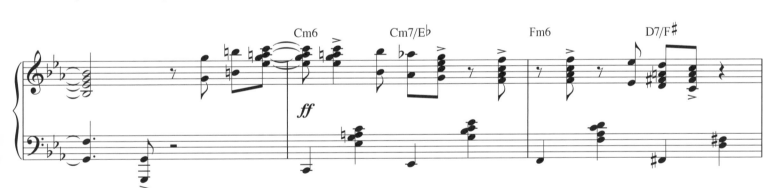

The Best-Selling Jazz Book of All Time Is Now Legal!

The Real Books are the most popular jazz books of all time. Since the 1970s, musicians have trusted these volumes to get them through every gig, night after night. The problem is that the books were illegally produced and distributed, without any regard to copyright law, or royalties paid to the composers who created these musical masterpieces.

Hal Leonard is very proud to present the first legitimate and legal editions of these books ever produced. You won't even notice the difference, other than all the notorious errors being fixed: the covers and typeface look the same, the song lists are nearly identical, and the price for our edition is even cheaper than the originals!

Every conscientious musician will appreciate that these books are now produced accurately and ethically, benefitting the songwriters that we owe for some of the greatest tunes of all time!

VOLUME 1
00240221	C Edition	$45.00
00240224	B♭ Edition	$45.00
00240225	E♭ Edition	$45.00
00240226	Bass Clef Edition	$45.00
00286389	F Edition	$39.99
00240292	C Edition 6 x 9	$39.99
00240339	B♭ Edition 6 x 9	$39.99
00147792	Bass Clef Edition 6 x 9	$39.99
00200984	Online Backing Tracks: Selections	$45.00
00110604	Book/USB Flash Drive Backing Tracks Pack	$85.00
00110599	USB Flash Drive Only	$50.00

VOLUME 2
00240222	C Edition	$45.00
00240227	B♭ Edition	$45.00
00240228	E♭ Edition	$45.00
00240229	Bass Clef Edition	$45.00
00240293	C Edition 6 x 9	$39.99
00125900	B♭ Edition 6 x 9	$39.99
00125900	The Real Book – Mini Edition	$39.99
00204126	Backing Tracks on USB Flash Drive	$50.00
00204131	C Edition – USB Flash Drive Pack	$85.00

VOLUME 3
00240233	C Edition	$45.00
00240284	B♭ Edition	$45.00
00240285	E♭ Edition	$45.00
00240286	Bass Clef Edition	$45.00
00240338	C Edition 6 x 9	$39.99

VOLUME 4
00240296	C Edition	$45.00
00103348	B♭ Edition	$45.00
00103349	E♭ Edition	$45.00
00103350	Bass Clef Edition	$45.00

VOLUME 5
00240349	C Edition	$45.00
00175278	B♭ Edition	$45.00
00175279	E♭ Edition	$45.00

VOLUME 6
00240534	C Edition	$45.00
00223637	E♭ Edition	$45.00

Also available:
00154230	The Real Bebop Book	$34.99
00240264	The Real Blues Book	$39.99
00310910	The Real Bluegrass Book	$39.99
00240223	The Real Broadway Book	$39.99
00240440	The Trane Book	$25.00
00125426	The Real Country Book	$45.00
00269721	The Real Miles Davis Book C Edition	$29.99
00269723	The Real Miles Davis Book B♭ Edition	$29.99
00240355	The Real Dixieland Book C Edition	$39.99
00294853	The Real Dixieland Book E♭ Edition	$39.99
00122335	The Real Dixieland Book B♭ Edition	$39.99
00240235	The Duke Ellington Real Book	$25.00
00240268	The Real Jazz Solos Book	$39.99
00240348	The Real Latin Book C Edition	$39.99
00127107	The Real Latin Book B♭ Edition	$39.99
00120809	The Pat Metheny Real Book C Edition	$34.99
00252119	The Pat Metheny Real Book B♭ Edition	$29.99
00240358	The Charlie Parker Real Book C Edition	$25.00
00275997	The Charlie Parker Real Book E♭ Edition	$25.00
00118324	The Real Pop Book – Vol. 1	$39.99
00240331	The Bud Powell Real Book	$25.00
00240437	The Real R&B Book C Edition	$45.00
00276590	The Real R&B Book B♭ Edition	$45.00
00240313	The Real Rock Book	$39.99
00240323	The Real Rock Book – Vol. 2	$39.99
00240359	The Real Tab Book	$39.99
00240317	The Real Worship Book	$35.00

THE REAL CHRISTMAS BOOK
00240306	C Edition	$35.00
00240345	B♭ Edition	$35.00
00240346	E♭ Edition	$35.00
00240347	Bass Clef Edition	$35.00
00240431	A-G CD Backing Tracks	$24.99
00240432	H-M CD Backing Tracks	$24.99
00240433	N-Y CD Backing Tracks	$24.99

THE REAL VOCAL BOOK
00240230	Volume 1 High Voice	$40.00
00240307	Volume 1 Low Voice	$40.00
00240231	Volume 2 High Voice	$39.99
00240308	Volume 2 Low Voice	$39.99
00240391	Volume 3 High Voice	$39.99
00240392	Volume 3 Low Voice	$39.99
00118318	Volume 4 High Voice	$39.99
00118319	Volume 4 Low Voice	$39.99

Complete song lists online at www.halleonard.com

HAL•LEONARD®

Prices, content, and availability subject to change without notice.

0422
318